# STRESS RELIEF
# DOG COLORING BOOK

For general information on our other products and services or to obtain technical support, please contact our Customer Care Department within the United States at (866) 744-2665, or outside the United States at (510) 253-0500.

Interior and Cover Designer: Lisa Schreiber
Art Producer: Hannah Dickerson
Editor: Brian Sweeting
Production Editor: Emily Sheehan
Illustrations © 2020 Collaborate Agency/Pimlada Phuapradit

ISBN: Print 978-1-64611-999-8
R0

# STRESS RELIEF
# DOG COLORING BOOK

**35** Detailed Designs for Adults

### ILLUSTRATED BY PIMLADA PHUAPRADIT

ROCKRIDGE
PRESS

# CONTENTS

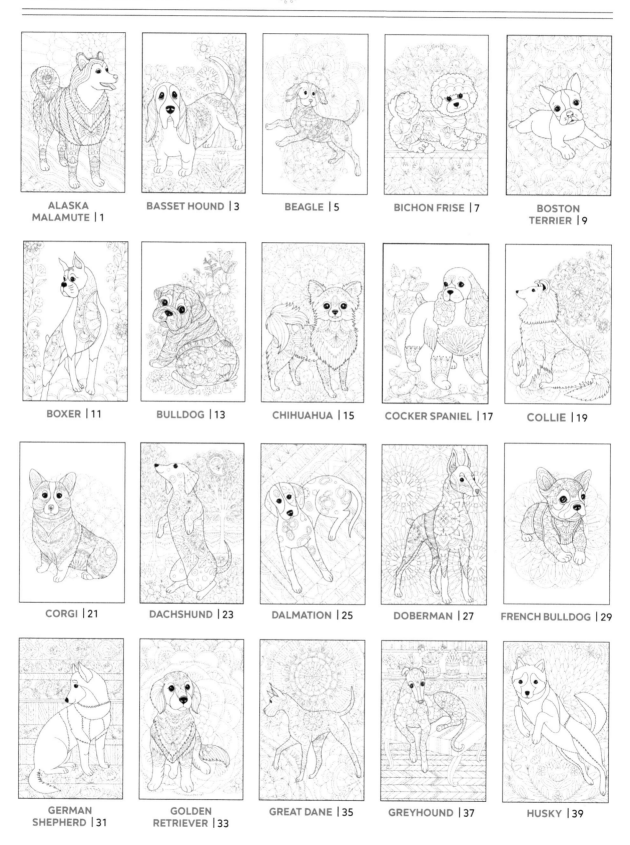

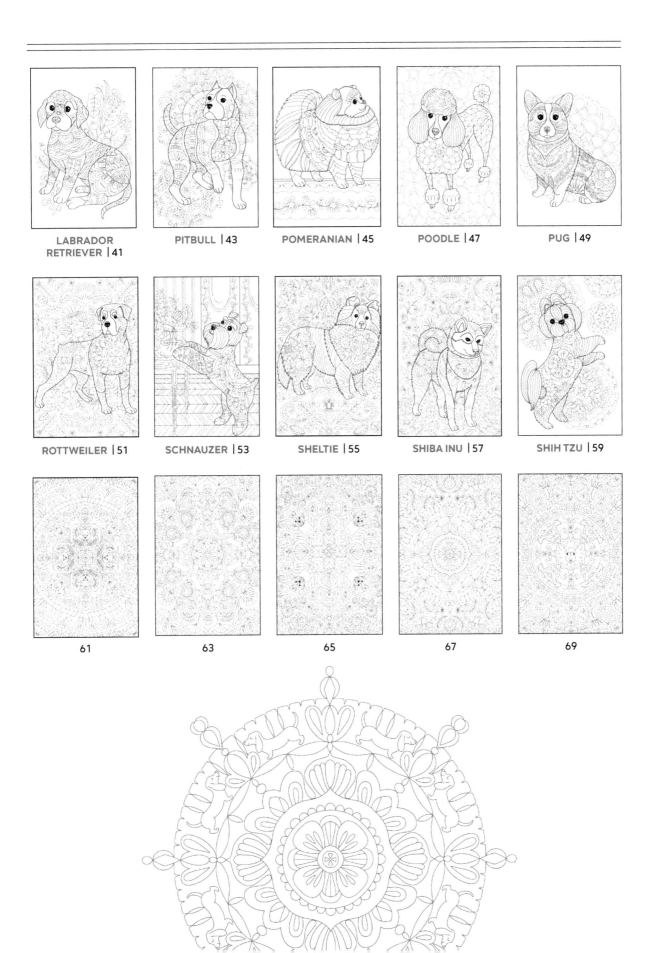

LABRADOR RETRIEVER |41

PITBULL |43

POMERANIAN |45

POODLE |47

PUG |49

ROTTWEILER |51

SCHNAUZER |53

SHELTIE |55

SHIBA INU |57

SHIH TZU |59

61

63

65

67

69

# ALASKAN MALAMUTE

BASSET HOUND

# BICHON FRISE

# BULLDOG

# CHIHUAHUA

# COCKER SPANIEL

COLLIE

.

DACHSHUND

# DALMATIAN

# DOBERMAN

# FRENCH BULLDOG

GERMAN SHEPHERD

GOLDEN RETRIEVER

GREYHOUND

# LABRADOR RETRIEVER

PITBULL

# POMERANIAN

POODLE

PUG

# ROTTWEILER

SCHNAUZER

SHELTIE

SHIBA INU

SHIH TZU

# ABOUT THE ARTIST

**PIMLADA PHUAPRADIT** is an illustrator and designer based in Thailand. Pim has loved to draw since she was a child and found the process of design and illustration to be an endless journey of fun experiments. She studied textile design at the Royal Melbourne Institute of Technology and then worked as a knitwear designer in Bangkok before pursuing further education in illustration as a visual essay at the School of Visual Arts. Her working process is a combination of hand-drawn and digital coloring. She enjoys researching details of textiles, vintage children's books, antique objects, and decorative elements of architecture.

CPSIA information can be obtained
at www.ICGtesting.com
Printed in the USA
JSHW052132110121
10823JS00004B/136